Computers and Technology

Explained to Nana and Papa

Computers and Technology

Explained to Nana and Papa

Steven C. Seow, Ph.D.

For Ethan and Madeleine

Contents

Preface

I have been working in a high-tech company in Washington State for over a dozen years. On my spare time, I write computer code, teach kids how to code, and fix computers and phones. I like to say that I am comfortable around computers and technology.

If you feel lost in all this modern-day computing, you are not alone. Computer technological advancements and inventions are accelerating so fast that even technical professionals in the field are getting lost when they don't pay attention to the emerging modern technology inventions.

Who is this for?

Fine, this is not just for *Nana* and *Papa*. This is for *anyone* who wants a succinct and practical overview and explanation of modern computer technologies that we find around us. These are readers who want to know enough about modern computing to be informed, safe, and productive.

Why did you write this book?

For years, I have been helping people around me understand how computer technology work and have inadvertently created a pile of notes, emails, messages, Facebook comments, and other online writeups. It occurred to me that if I were to compile all the knowledge into a book, it can be given to someone who will find it useful.

What motivates me more to write this book is the unavoidable malevolence that comes with these modern technologies, which are almost always invented and developed with the intent to make the work and life more productive, and the world better and safer.

Unscrupulous characters will have very little hesitation to use technology to exploit other people's fear or kindness, almost always for monetary gains.

Just for my readers, I am extending a one-time offer to buy Bitcoin at 75% off for a limited time! A dozen of these magnificent newly-minted gold-plated Bitcoin for only $500. Half of the proceeds will go to some starving children. Want to buy some?

I don't claim to have a panacea for all the malice in the tech world but being and staying informed is the good start and a great first line of defense.

How is this book organized?

The book starts with a few chapters covering the basic home computer hardware, like desktops and laptops. I will also talk about the millions of smart devices that we find in homes today.

With every machine, device, and appliance come problems, and with problems come maintenance, repairs, upgrades, replacements, etc. I devote a chapter on that so that you can be informed on the options that are available and what to avoid.

We will also dive into the world of the Internet, software, and websites, and take a quick look at the modern apps and popular online services (like Facebook, Instagram, Snapchat, etc.) on their use and how they work.

In any ecosystem, there are always bad actors, so I'll cover security related topics such as passwords, viruses, and other really well-thought-out technologies that are designed to help keep you and your information safe.

The book concludes with a chapter devoted to the latest shiny stuff in the world of tech, what they are, and how they may affect the way you communicate, do your banking, manage your data, etc.

Disclaimer

This is not a complete historical account of computers. This is also not a guide on how to use a specific software or hardware. The views and opinions are mine and do not reflect or endorse any company or product.

I expect to release a newer edition of this book frequently enough to keep up with the latest technology and trends that are most likely relevant to you, so I welcome feedback and suggestions for topics. I invite you to email me at sseow@hotmail.com.

Chapter 1

Companies & Brand Names

One of the reasons to have this chapter is because company names, brand names, product names, and technology names are frequently used interchangeably, which can be very confusing to some users.

You are typing something on your *Microsoft 360* that is newly installed your *Dell* hard drive, and you realized that you need to go to the *Google* to find some information, right?

Hmm... not quite.

I don't blame you. Some tech companies can't seem to get naming and branding quite

right. Let's untangle this mess by pulling out
the company names as a start.

Microsoft

Microsoft is a Redmond-based company that
makes software products (like *Office* and
Windows) and hardware (like *Surface* laptop
and the *Xbox*) among other products and
online services in its big portfolio.

Bill Gates is one of two names that people
typically associate with Microsoft. The other
is the late **Paul Allen**. Microsoft products and
services can either be a one-time purchase or
a subscription.

It is common to see the name of some
Microsoft products preceded by the company
name, such as *Microsoft Windows*. Others
may not bear the company name, such as
Office 365. No one buys a copy of *Microsoft*
to install on a laptop. You are probably
referring to a copy of Microsoft Windows.
Some of their products, namely *Microsoft*

Office, are really a collection or a **suite** of software programs. In this case, you will find the popular *Microsoft Word*, *Microsoft PowerPoint*, and others in the suite. You won't be using *Microsoft Office* to type up a letter; you'll be using *Microsoft Word,* which is one of the products in Microsoft Office suite.

Apple

Apple is a Cupertino-based company founded by the late **Steve Jobs**. The company makes hardware (like the *iPhone* and *MacBook*) and with a few exceptions, the software that runs on their hardware. Other companies, including Microsoft, do make software that runs on Apple phones and computers as well. However, no companies are allowed to build hardware that runs Apple's proprietary operating systems. We'll cover operating systems in another chapter.

Apple has a knack for naming some of their products with the signature lowercase "i" prefix, such as *iPhone*, *iPad*, *iPod*, *iCloud*, and *iTunes*. Their leading money maker is the iPhones, which accounts for almost 60% of its revenue. Their logo is the unmistakable apple with a bite taken off it on the right side of the fruit. *i*Like!

SOME OF APPLE'S FLAGSHIP PRODUCTS.

Google

Google is a Mountain View-based company founded by two Stanford University students, **Larry Page** and **Sergey Brin**. Besides giving us the world's most popular search engine, *Google.com*, they have many other outstanding web-based services, notably *Gmail* and *YouTube*. They are also in the hardware business, with a smartphone line and laptop line branded *Pixel*.

Other than the famed search engine (which accounts for 86% of its revenue), another popular Google product is their Internet browser, *Chrome*. We will go into the distinction between a search engine and an Internet browser in a later chapter. Another popular product that would make the top 10 products made by Google is *Android*, which runs the non-Apple smartphones you see these days.

Fun fact: Versions of Android are named alphabetically after snacks: *Oreo, Nougat, Marshmallow, Lollipop, KitKat, Jelly Bean,* etc.

Amazon

Amazon is a Seattle-based company founded by **Jeff Bezos**, the richest man in the world. Amazon may have started out selling books, but today its portfolio of businesses spans both hardware and software, and into non-high-tech industries as well, including *Amazon Fresh* (groceries delivery), *Amazon Go* (brick and mortar grocery store), and *Amazon Prime* (subscription-based service that includes benefits like free shipping, streaming movies, etc.)

Amazon continues to surprise us with the different types of products and services, but their leading revenue stream is their online retail behemoth, *Amazon.com*, which accounts for about two-thirds of their revenue.

Chapter 2

Operating Systems

Before we go into the differences between a desktop and a laptop in the next few chapters, we should talk about the special software that makes them run.

The operating system (abbreviated **OS**) is what makes a device operational and allows us to install apps, games, and other *peripherals* (like printers, keyboard, mouse etc.) on it.

Think of the OS like the collection of plumbing, wires, and other critical components that goes into a house. The apps, games, and other stuff we add into a computer are like the appliances.

If an app or game has a serious problem, chances are other parts of the computer will continue work. However, if the OS has a serious problem, chances are nothing will work. Back to our house analogy: if the water to the house is shut off, the bathrooms, washer, and water faucets in the kitchen sinks aren't going to work.

Every computer will have an operating system. The more popular ones that you should have heard of is **Windows** (made by Microsoft) and **Mac** (short for *Macintosh*, made by Apple). The latter typically refer to both the Apple computers as well as its operating system. The operating system is more accurately called **macOS.**

The combination of a desktop or a laptop running Windows is frequently referred to as a **PC** or **personal computer**. While not entirely accurate, it has become the way to distinguish between a Windows-based computer from a MacOS-based computer. So, if you will hear someone ask if you have "Windows or Mac" or "PC or Mac", you know what it means.

Smartphones and other devices need operating systems as well. Samsung phones, for example, are likely running on the **Android OS** (developed by Google) and Apple's iPhones and iPads run on **iOS**.

Operating systems have versions, and each new version is supposed to be better, more secure, and more capable. Keep in mind that when a new version of an operating system is released, it is considered an **upgrade** from the previous version, which is a new product altogether.

What you need to know

When the company decides to release a smaller add-on to fix particular issues, it is typically referred to as an **update**. Updates are typically free. Unless the company is releasing operating systems for free, upgrades will need to be purchased.

Talking about updates… every operating system will typically have the capability to update itself over the Internet. This means that there is no need to have the company send you a new DVD, go purchase an update, or pay someone to do it for you (unless you are truly uncomfortable in doing so).

Most OS's will have an option that allows you to set an automatic download and installation of updates without requiring you to do anything. A few may actually perform updates without telling you. The rest will allow you to click a button to check for updates. This is what you find on your smartphone and tablets. If there are one or more updates, you have the choice to download and install it.

It is a good practice to check and install the latest operating system and software updates available because that is how the software manufacturers fix newly discovered security issues that a hacker may exploit. Additionally, updates are also used to fix **software bugs**. We'll cover bugs in another chapter.

Another important thing to know is that certain OS's may only work on certain computers. For example, you can't run Apple's macOS on a Dell laptop. Chances are the Dell computers you find on the shelves run Windows (or another OS called *Chrome OS*). There is also a chance you can't run (at least properly) newer versions of an OS on a much older computer.

Whether the new version of a software program or app will run on an older hardware is sometimes referred to as **backwards compatibility**. Most peripherals and software are designed to work only with certain versions of an operating system. On the packaging or website, you may find this listed under some heading like **minimum requirements**.

Windows

At the time of writing, the latest version of Windows is **Windows 10**. Generally, you will find the Windows operating system (first released in 1985) running on common brand name computers like Dell, HP, Acer, Asus, Toshiba, Lenovo, and others. Some versions before Windows 10 are *Windows 8*, *Windows 7*, *Windows Vista*, and *Windows XP*. Just to put things into perspective, *Windows XP* dates back to 2003.

What you need to know

Remember that companies like Dell manufactures the hardware but they do not develop the operating system. This may partially explain why the customer support at HP is not willing or able to help you with how you can turn off that pesky screensaver – it's really the operating system's problem. They'll likely tell you to call Microsoft.

That said, when you buy a complete computer at retailers like Costco or BestBuy, you typically pay one price that includes both the machine (desktop or laptop) and the installed operating system.

You can, of course, choose to buy and install another version or edition operating system. Windows 10 (and other software for that matter), for example, has different editions, like *Home* or *Pro editions,* that have differences in the features and capabilities.

Manufacturers like Dell typically have an agreement with Microsoft to only sell their computers with the latest version of Windows. This is why you will not be able to find retailers selling brand-new Dell laptops running Windows 7 or 8.

One of the pros of Windows is how widely-used it is. At the time of writing, it has 4 times more users than Apple's Mac platform, or about **400 million** just on Windows 10 alone. Because of this, you will find most, it not all, of the desktop apps you need to use on a laptop or desktop. Additionally, having different hardware manufacturers means lower prices and more options for the consumers.

One of the cons of Windows is... how widely-used it is! Hackers like to pick a target that will yield the biggest "returns". In other words, it is more (negatively) impactful to hack a platform that has 100 million users than to hack one that has 10.

Does that mean that Windows is an unsafe operating system to use? Absolutely not. There are recommendations and other good practices that will give you a safe personal computing using Windows. We'll cover that in another chapter!

Macs

Mac typically refers to both the hardware and operating system developed by **Apple**. The operating system is called *macOS* and it runs exclusively on Apple's Mac products: **MacBook's** (their laptop line) and **iMacs** (their desktop line). We'll go into the hardware in the next section.

Fun fact: Versions of macOS come in beautiful codenames like *macOS Mojave* (at the time of writing) or *El Capitan* or *High Sierra*. Behind the scenes, there is actually a numerical version as well. For example, Mojave is really macOS 10.14.

What you need to know

Apple computers can only run software (apps, games, etc.) that are specially developed for it. That is, if you have a DVD or CD that has a photo management app that is designed for Windows, you will not be able to install and use it on a Mac. Many software developers will create two versions of their app – one for Windows and one for Mac.

Two of the pros of Mac computers are their beautiful design and stability, largely due to the blessing that it is one company designing both the hardware and the software. Apple is known to maintain high design and engineering standards, and it shows. It is also less of a target for hackers and that alone is one of the biggest reasons new users are drawn to Mac.

One of the biggest cons is price. At the time of writing, the entry level laptop will cost you $1,299. There are a few other little limitations that makes it less ideal than Windows. Some gaming enthusiasts, for example, will find a scarcity in game titles. This is generally true for other software as well: there is just more on the Windows platform.

Chrome OS

Not to be mistaken for the Internet browser, *Chrome* is also the name of an operating system developed by Google. The relatively newer operating system is found in small desktops called *Chrome boxes* and laptops called *Chromebooks*, made by manufacturers like Dell, Acer, Asus, Toshiba, and HP. We will visit Chromebooks in the laptop chapter.

Mobile OS

Yes, your smartphone needs an operating system as well. In fact, all mobile devices do. That electronic parking meter with the touch screen you see in the city needs an operating system as well.

On iPhones and iPads, the operating system is Apple's **iOS**. On non-Apple phones, like Samsung or LG, it's likely Android although you may still find some smartphones running a mobile version of Windows on the discontinued Windows Phones.

All mobile operating system platforms have specific ways by which you install apps (short for applications), so it will be difficult to make a mistake on which version to choose. That said, sometimes it is possible to install apps in alternate ways. This is sometimes referred to as *sideloading*. Sometimes you will see the word *jailbreak* to describe phones or devices that have been modified to allow for the sideloading of apps or extra functionalities. Manufacturers usually don't like this and I typically recommend against it.

Both iOS and Android have all the apps you will ever need, so the choice really boils down to other factors like price and design. There will have a chapter devoted to smartphones.

Chapter 3

Desktop Computers

Depending on who you ask, desktop computers were invented in the 1960s or 1970s. Today, when we say *desktop*, we are typically referring to that bulky metallic briefcase-sized machine sitting on or under your desk.

Depending on its size, that metallic enclosure is sometimes referred to as a **tower**. A regular desktop tower would likely weigh upwards of 20 lbs., so it is not something you would carry into Starbucks! That would likely be a laptop.

There are smaller and slimmer desktops. The term **form factor** refers to the size and shape of the desktop. Some small form factor desktops (sometimes called **micro desktops**) are as small as a thick paperback.

If you were to open up a desktop, you are going to find the components that are required to make it hum. You will see a lot of colored cables, fans, integrated chips modules, motherboards, shiny stuff… thankfully, you don't have to know them all.

There are just a few things you should know to help you select a desktop for purchase, or to purchase a replacement or upgrade part. Let's take a closer look at some of these components of the desktop.

Hard Drives

Some people have mistaken the desktop for the *hard drive*. The common hard disk drives (abbreviated **HDD**) are roughly the size of a credit card or wallet, and anywhere from about 0.4 inches to about an inch in thickness. Its job is to store data, like the photos and music that you keep on your computer.

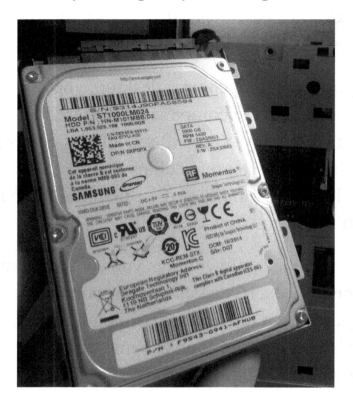

A TYPICAL CONVENTIONAL HARD DISK DRIVE

Hard drives are primarily measured by how much data they can hold. These are in units of **GB (gigabyte)** or **TB (terabyte)**. 1,000 GB makes up 1 TB. For normal use, a 250 GB might be more than enough. If you are looking to store a lot of images or videos, then looking at 500 GB or 1TB hard disk drives might more appropriate.

For a frame of reference, a picture from taken from your phone might be around 2 to 3 **MB** (**megabyte**). You will need about 300 of these pictures to take up 1 GB of disk space, or 300,000 pictures to take up 1 TB.

Conventional hard disk drives use moving needles that read and write data on multiple disks, very much like vinyl records on classic record player. Think of *reading* as playback and *writing* as recording. This needle-and-disk technology is found in the majority of our hard drive running in our desktops today.

There's some bad news.

When you save some data like a picture into your hard disk drive, the data making up the picture is recorded (or written) onto the disk. When the operating system cannot find an empty spot on the disk to write the entire data in one piece, what it will do instead is to break the data into many locations all over the disk.

When it is time to *read* the file (say, you are looking up a baby picture), the needles will have to move to several locations just to read one baby picture. When you have thousands of files stored this way, the needle is furiously moving all over the disks.

Because of this and other moving parts, these drives are prone to mechanical failures. In fact, these drives are expected to last about 3 to 5 years before showing signs of failure. On average, 20% of hard disk drives are expected to fail in the fourth year.

A newer alternative to these conventional disk drives is what is called **Solid State Drive** (abbreviated **SSD**). Unlike the conventional ones, these drives do not have moving parts which makes them less prone to mechanical failure. They also use less power and run about 30% faster.

Well, why don't we just switch over to SSD then? Well, the biggest hurdle is that they are easily five times more expensive than HDD.

SSD should not be mistaken for **external hard disk drives** (or **external HDD**), which are really just a hard drive (may be the conventional type or SSD type) inside an enclosure that can be attached to and detached from your desktop or laptop. These external drives typically are connected into a USB port on your computer and function great for large files and backups.

Memory

Memory is different than storage. While storage refers to how much information the desktop can store, memory refers to how much it can move or process at a time. It is common to see memory described as **RAM** or a specific type of computer called the *Random Access Memory*.

THE INSIDE OF A LAPTOP SHOWING A SINGLE MEMORY MODULE INSTALLED. MOST MEMORY MODULES ARE GREEN IN COLOR.

Memory is measured in gigabyte or GB (same unit as the HDD) in even numbers like 4, 8, or 16 GB. A low-end desktop and laptop should have at least 4 GB of memory, but 8 and 16 GB are getting common and are highly recommended. 32 GB is great.

Memory directly impacts how fast your computer runs apps and games. As an example, if you were to use a small car to move your belongings from one house to another, you will take a much longer time than if you were to use a large moving truck.

The volume of belongings in the house remains the same.

What you need to know

When the computer starts to slow down, it is not because the memory chips are getting old or weak. In fact, any slight electronic hiccup with the memory chips will likely cause the entire device to not work. It is more likely that the burden placed on the memory has gotten larger so now it has to do more with the same amount of resources.

This could be the result of more apps that have been installed since you got the computer, or perhaps a newer version of an app that now demands more memory to be functional.

Unlike tablets and phones, memory for a desktop and laptop are frequently upgradable – meaning that you can increase the memory to make the computer run faster. That said, each computer is designed to accommodate up to a maximum amount of memory.

Memory comes in flat rectangular IC or integrated circuit modules about an inch in width and about 3 to 5 inches in length. Although they look all the same, memory modules come in different sizes, types and speeds, so it is important that compatible ones are used.

Computer Ports

At the back of the desktop, it is not common to find a myriad of **ports** (many of which you may never use!) It is common to find some commonly-used ports at the front of the desktop as well. Ports or jacks are how your **peripherals**, such as keyboard, mouse, speakers, monitors, external drives, etc. are connected to the computer.

Many desktop problems are due to a cable becoming loose from a port or jack, especially if the desktop was physically moved. These ports are designed with a specific size and shape, and connectors on cables that are plugged into them are designed to fit securely and not detach with a light tug. We'll talk about general computer issues in a later chapter.

BACK OF A DESKTOP SHOWING A VARIETY OF PORTS AND JACKS. YOU WILL VERY LIKELY END UP USING ONLY SOME OF THESE.

The most common ports that you need to know about are the ones that supply **power** to the desktop, the one that goes to the back of your monitor for **video**, the **ethernet** port for network connection, and the **audio** jacks for sound, and the **USB** ports.

Power

On a desktop, the power port should look familiar and almost always has three metal prongs and is usually black in color. Chances are it is located at the back and top of the desktop (if the desktop stands upright) and is most likely the biggest port you see back there.

The power cable, also typically black in color, should be plugged firmly into this power port and the end of the cable should be plugged into a standard power outlet. Yes, if that power cable looks familiar, it is a standard domestic NEMA power cord used for many household appliances.

Video

The video port is used to send video signals from your desktop to a monitor. These video parts are commonly found in the back of the desktop. If they are conveniently labeled, you may see abbreviations like **VGA**, **DVI**, or **HDMI**. These are different types of video ports (and there are others), each using a different type of cable and each supporting different levels of **display resolutions**.

THE BACK OF A COMPUTER MONITOR SHOWING THE POWER PORT (LEFT), A HDMI (TOP LEFT), AUDIO OUT (TOP RIGHT), A DVI (WHITE, BOTTOM LEFT), AND VGA (BLUE, BOTTOM RIGHT)

Display resolutions are shown in two numbers, like 1,600 x 900, which indicate that width and height in **pixels**. These numbers, along with the **screen size** (measured in inches from one corner to the diagonally-opposite corner) decides how crisp and clear things look on the screen of your monitor. Just in case you heard of the term **4k** used to describe monitors and TVs, that simply means *ultra-high definition* video displayed with a resolution of at least 3,840 x 2,160. If your life or line of work demands skin pore clarity and cinematic quality, knock yourself out.

It is possible to use more than one video port if or when you want to use more than one monitor. Which video port you use depends a lot on what your monitor is capable of. You will find ports at the back of your monitor as well. Many desktops these days use the DVI type. Older monitors will certainly have the VGA port, which commonly has a blue-colored port.

One thing that you may notice is how some cable connectors, like the ones found on the DVI cable, have two screws that you can use to fasten the plug into the port. I highly recommend using these to secure the connector and prevent it from becoming loose.

USB

Invented in the late 90s, USB (**Universal Serial Bus**) is perhaps the most commonly used port today. There is a plethora of computer **peripherals**, like webcam, keyboard, mouse, printer, speakers, microphones, etc. that use USB. There are even novelty USB devices like mug warmers, mini fans, small vacuums, and decorative neon signs.

Needless to say, because they are designed to give out some voltage, one of the most common use for the USB ports is to charge a device like a smartphone. That said, without

going into electrical engineering, be prepared
for a longer time to get to a full charge on
your smartphone using your computer's USB
port.

**BACK OF A DESKTOP SHOWING 5 AVAILABLE USB PORTS WITH
A NETWORK PORT.**

In 2008, a new version of USB was released.
While it looks exactly the same physically,
USB 3.0 or SuperSpeed USB, are designed
to be 10 times faster than its predecessor.
Faster in this context means the speed at
which it moves information.

What does that mean really? Well, if it takes
10 seconds to copy a picture from your

desktop to, say, a USB thumb drive, with USB 3.0, it will only take 1 second.

You can easily spot a USB 3.0 port or cable because it typically blue in color on the inside. In fact, manufacturers are supposed to use the Pantone 300C color.

Remember that there is a logical side to the USB port. That is, a USB cable should only be able to fit correctly with correct side up.

If you ever see a tiny fingernail-sized USB thingamajig plugged into a USB port, do not panic. Chances are the receivers that allow some peripheral (commonly, keyboard and mouse) to work with your desktop wirelessly.

Ethernet

Next up is the port that is used for Internet access. The **ethernet** port, sometimes labeled **LAN,** looks very much like a telephone port but wider. For those who might have spent time in telecommunications, the landline phone system uses the RJ11. The ethernet port and cable uses a wider RJ45.

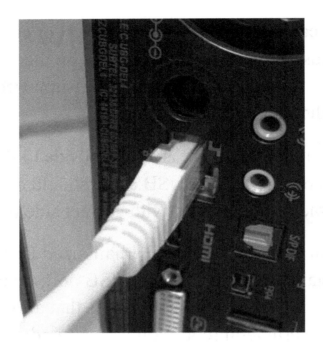

AN ETHERNET CABLE IS SHOWN PLUGGED INTO AN ETHERNET PORT

When the cable is inserted correctly, you should hear a click (just like the ones on the landline phone). If you don't, either a tiny plastic piece has broken off (very common) or you have it upside down. The cable is still functional but it will not be secure and will likely pop out with the slightest movement.

To release, do not yank! Make sure you pinch that tiny plastic protrusion called the lock release clip.

As mentioned, a frequent network connection problem is related to the connector becoming loose. For ethernet ports and cables, there should be one or two blinking or steady LED lights on the port itself to tell you if it is receiving any signal.

There is no significance to the color of the ethernet cable itself. Once in a blue moon (no pun intended), you find an ethernet cable (sometimes called a CAT5 or CAT5e) that doesn't quite work because it is a crossover cable.

We don't need to go into when these are used but it should be easy to spot a crossover cable by comparing the jacks on both ends. If you look carefully at the clear RJ45 connector, you will see 8 color-coded wires. For the more common or *straight though* CAT5 cable, the sequence of the colors of the wires are identical. A cross-cover cable will have the color sequence reversed on one of the connectors.

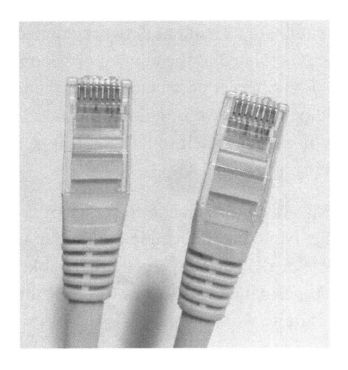

Sometimes, the cable doesn't function correctly because it was intended for specific uses. Some of these cables may not have all the eight wires utilized.

Audio

The next set of common computer ports is the **audio** ports or jack. These are the ports responsible for producing or receiving audio for your software, videos, games, etc.

Most commonly, you will see at least two, if not three, color-coded circular 3.5mm jacks: pink, light blue, and green. The **pink** is typically used for a microphone, the **light blue** for audio input, and the **green** for sound output. This last one, the green, is where you will plug in your headphones or powered speakers.

Some newer speakers will use USB ports, so you may not need bother with these audio ports at all. Others with advanced sound systems may use the larger RCA jacks, have more ports to accommodate surround sound, or use optical cables for digital audio outputs.

Chapter 4

Laptops

Compared to desktops, laptops have a wider variation in terms of operating system, capability, etc. While their main purpose is be portable computers, it is not uncommon for people to use them as home computers.

Windows Laptops

Windows laptops are very common and there is no significant difference between the Windows running on a desktop and on a laptop. Some people distinguish laptops from **notebooks**, a term that is hardly used these days. A few years back, there was a momentary peak in **netbooks**, which are noticeably smaller and less powerful than a laptop. For the rest of this chapter, we'll just call them **laptops**.

You will find some of the ports described in the previous chapter on a laptop as well, but fewer. The power port for a laptop is typically located at the back or side of the laptop. This is commonly circular in shape and is a frequent cause of battery charging issues.

The most commonly used port on a laptop is probably the USB port. You may also find video ports that will allow you to connect your laptop to a monitor. Color coding of ports found in desktops are similar in older laptops, but newer models may not have ports that aren't color coded.

Occasionally, a laptop manufacturer will provide a *dongle* to provide additional ports, especially if the laptop is intended to be slim. Yes, apparently, some laptops suffer from body image issues. They are called, believe it or not, *ultra-thin* or *ultra-light* laptops.

Battery Life

Unlike desktops, laptops can run without constant power supply because they have a rechargeable battery. Due to the chemistry of the battery cells, these batteries aren't designed to recharged and used forever. Most laptop batteries will start to "fail" after 2 years or so, or **about 400** recharges or cycles.

Past that point, the battery's ability to hold its charge (more technically, its *capacity*) will decrease. You can tell when this is happening when the battery power depletes and recharges much quicker than before. At the top corner of the Windows or Mac desktop, you will typically see a percentage indicating how much battery life is left. Watch how fast this percentage drops (without having the laptop plugged in) and climbs (when you have it plugged in and charging).

Yes, you read right: Don't be happy when your laptop takes a shorter time to get to a full charge. It is sign that it is not performing correctly, and it is time for a replacement.

Older laptop models have detachable batteries, which makes it easy for you to replace them or carry around a spare. Newer laptops are integrating their batteries under the hood, which means that you will need to remove them tiny screws to get to them. They are still replaceable but you will definitely need a pair of steady hand to do so.

Types of Laptops

Laptop manufacturers have gotten creative in their design over the years. The typical laptops open and close like a book with a keyboard on one side and a screen on the other. Now, you will find screens that will flip or twist in unnatural angles to allow you to hold and use it like a clipboard. Then there are several models that have **detachable screens**, essentially turning the screen into a tablet.

THESE TWO SURFACE LAPTOPS FROM MICROSOFT HAVE DETACHABLE SCREENS.

The pros of a laptop are clear: It is light and you can bring it anywhere. There are, needless to say, some limitations and constraints when you compare a laptop to a desktop.

For example, it is not possible to upgrade the video graphics card of a laptop or its screen size. Typically, the bigger the screen (measured diagonally), the pricier the laptop. It is also more challenging (if possible at all) to upgrade components in a laptop. Keyboard layouts on a laptop typically can't match the generous full-sized keyboards that you would use with a desktop (although you can always use a separate keyboard with a laptop).

Fun Fact: You may have heard of people developing Carpal Tunnel Syndrome in their wrist because of prolonged keyboard use. Research data shows that that is probably not true.

A less obvious con in laptops is ergonomics. When placed on a desk (or worst, on your lap), chances are you will be slouching or bending the neck unnaturally just to see the screen properly. Thankfully, there are laptop stands that you can buy to elevate its height to accommodate a better posture.

MacBooks

MacBooks are Apple laptops. No other manufacturer makes laptops that run Apple's macOS. There are three general types of MacBooks: the regular *MacBook*, *MacBook*

Air, and *MacBook Pro*. Each differ in its *technical specifications* or its screen size, how much memory and storage space it has, etc., but all have that signature sleek metallic look.

The keyboard on a Mac looks about the same as the ones found on a Windows-based laptop with some slight differences. You will find some keys on a Mac keyboard that you will not find on a PC keyboard. For example, you will find the *Cmd* or *Command key* ⌘ only on the Mac keyboard. Some seasoned Windows users will also find some minor differences in the way you navigate, such as vertical scrolling on the touchpad.

Fun fact: There is no *backspace* key on the Mac keyboard! The *delete* key on the Mac works like the backspace key on PCs.

There are good reasons why many tout the Mac as a safer laptop or operating system in general, but there isn't a laptop that is 100% immune to computer viruses. So, yes, a Mac can get infected although less likely than a Windows-based computer.

Chromebooks

Chromebooks are laptops that run Google's Chrome OS. On the outside, they look identical to a laptop running Windows.

A software that is designed for Windows, say, Office, will not run on a Chromebook. Google's philosophy on the use of Chromebooks is very cloud-oriented: what you need to do should be in the *cloud*: checking Facebook, checking email, surfing the web. However, if you're hoping to do some photo editing using *Adobe Photoshop,* you may be out of luck. As such, a limitation in Chromebooks today is the availability of apps at least for now.

A very clear pro in Chromebooks is the price. It is not uncommon to find Chromebooks in the $200 to $300 range. If you primarily need a laptop to surf the web, check emails, etc., Chromebook is a perfect choice.

Gaming desktops and laptops

A class of desktops and laptops deserves its own section. Gaming desktops and laptops aren't hard to spot: they are typically spaceship-like or sinister-looking and cost two to five times more than a regular desktop. At the time of writing, you are probably looking at around $1,500 to $3,000 for a basic gaming desktop. Costco features a gaming desktop that goes for $6,000.

Just for clarity, gaming here refers to computer games and gaming computers are typically required for extremely visually-rich games like *role-playing games* (abbreviated *RPG*) or *first-person shooter games* (abbreviated *FPSG*). Here, we throw in another gaming acronym: *MMO – massively multiplayer online game.*

Why are these gaming systems so expensive? Apart of aesthetics, gaming computers typically use the most powerful components in order to maximize the gaming experience. A top-of-the-line graphics card used by the computer to render visuals in the game very quickly and very realistically can cost just about a regular desktop. Other components that contribute to the overall high cost include parts like memory, processor, special power supply, special cooling systems, etc.

Because of these high-end parts, most gaming laptops end up being bigger and bulkier than the non-gaming one. Razer, a gaming system maker, sells a fully-loaded $4,000 gaming laptop that weighs about 6.7 lbs.

Non-gaming desktops and laptops are still capable of playing most games, so you do not need a gaming laptop just to play Solitaire or other *casual games*. The question is how demanding the game is. If the requirements of the game are too high, it will likely degrade the visual quality of the game or not install at all.

All-in-One

All-in-One (or whatever each manufacturer calls their line) refers to a desktop system that seem to have no separate tower: only a monitor and its peripheral, or so it seems. The hardware concept is not new. One can argue that Apple was the first to come up with such a hybrid device with their *iMac* in 1998.

The guts of this hybrid system are tucked into the back or the base of the monitor. Because the components are so slim, they really look more like laptop components then desktop components.

All-in-One's are great space savers but they are as difficult to upgrade as a laptop due to the limited space that the manufacturers have to work with. Some All-in-One's are absolutely gorgeous and absolutely expensive. Microsoft's *Surface Studio 2* exceeds $4,000. Apple's *iMac Pro* with loaded bells and whistles can reach north of $13,000.

Chapter 5

Smartphones

Ah, yes... clever phones. These pocket computers are dominated by two operating system platforms in the U.S: Apple's **iPhone** and **Android** phones that can run on a variety of hardware manufacturers, namely, Samsung.

Smartphones are either a blessing or a curse to our generation, but one thing is for sure: they are here to stay. Each newer version of a smartphone seem to get faster, thinner, brighter, more battery life... and according to some recent news, soon they will even be bendable.

In the meantime, there really isn't much that can be done with upgrading smartphones since each components and circuitry are painstaking designed. So, if you find your smartphone slowing down, increasing its memory is NOT going to be an option.

Most smartphones are advertised with a *storage* capacity (like 32 GB, 64 GB, 128 GB, 256 GB and so on) NOT the *memory* capacity. Some phones may come with an option to add additional storage capacity by using **MicroSD cards** which looks about the size of a fingernail or smaller.

The only advice I have is to purchase the model with the best configuration that you value, like screen size, battery life, camera quality, and storage space.

Moving parts on a smartphone are minimal, which helps reduce issues related to mechanical parts. That said, some cameras on smartphones have high-end cameras that make minor mechanical adjustments for focusing and, once in a while, there may be mechanical failures related to that.

Battery

First introduced by Sony in 1991, *lithium-ion* batteries in smartphones are expected to last 2 to 3 years. To prolong the battery life, experts recommend letting the phone run very low before recharging. In most instances, these batteries in modern smartphones can be replaced.

Online retailers, like Amazon.com, sell aftermarket batteries for most smartphone models, but how easy it is to replace them is another question. Without going into details, the batteries in iPhones are easier to replace than the ones in the newer Android-based smart phones.

What you need to know

If your smartphone starts to charge too quickly and use power too quickly, it is definitely time to get a new battery. This can be done at home by purchasing a replacement kit from Amazon, but great care should be taken as the connectors and other components inside the smartphones are extremely delicate.

If you are brave enough to replace your own smartphone battery, you want to make sure you select one that is compatible and to go for the highest *milliamp hour* (abbreviated **mAh)** you can find. The mAh is a measure of how long a battery can power the phone on a full charge. Technically, this is called a *discharge.* For example, a 4,000 mAh battery will theoretically last twice as long as one rated at 2,000 mAh.

Remember that smartphone batteries are extremely flammable if punctured. This is one of the reasons why we are always encouraged to dispose batteries properly. There has been a recent famous case of faulty batteries causing more chaos.

Smartphone batteries can malfunction and overheat. When a smartphone feels abnormally hot to the touch, it is time to stop using the phone and have it checked out. The next possible phase after overheating is for the battery to physically swell.

THE PHONE BATTERY AT THE BACK THAT HAS VISIBLE SIGNS OF SWELLING. THE ONE NEXT TO IT IS A NORMAL ONE THAT HASN'T SWELLED.

The swelling typically causes pressure inside-out and will soon start to pop a screen or an edge of the phone, or cause patches of discoloration on the screen. In either case, it is certainly time to stop using the phone.

Not So Fun Fact: In 2016, the batteries in Samsung's *Galaxy Note 7* were exploding, prompting the company to recall the phones worldwide. It was reported that 96% of 3 million Note 7's sold were recalled.

Data Backup

Data is saved into storage in phones very much like how it is done in computers. It is always a good practice to **backup** (save duplicate copies) the data from your smartphone regularly. Otherwise, if the phone is damaged beyond repair, the wedding and baby pictures in the phone will be lost forever.

There are several ways to save the pictures, videos, or other data from the phone. A possible way is to use the manufacturer's prescribed method to do a **backup**. For iPhone, for example, there is a backup feature in *iTunes*, a software application that installed on your computer. This usually requires that the iPhone be plugged into a USB port of a computer that has iTunes installed.

When it becomes necessary to put the data back on the phone or a new phone, the process is typically called a **restore**. For most phones, once the computer recognizes the phone, it may even be possible to copy the files like you would from a hard disk drive.

There is also a *cloud* approach where files are saved into cloud, such as *iCloud* for iPhones. This approach does become unrealistic if you already have a lot of photos and videos because it will take an awfully long time for the backup to be completed.

Besides using the cloud and plugging (or more accurately, **tethering**) the phone into a computer using a USB cable, there are some gadget options as well. *SanDisk*, a storage device company, for example, sells flash drives that you can plug directly into the smartphone and with the help of an app, extract your data directly into the storage device.

Phone Repairs

By far, the predominant issue that people have with their smartphones is breaking the screen. The screens on both iPhone and

Android-based phones are replaceable, so don't buy a new phone just because you have a cracked screen.

Some network carriers and manufacturers, like Apple, offer service and insurance plans to repair your phone at a lower rate. Apple calls their **AppleCare**+ which can cover screen replacements at $30.

There are plenty of other places to bring in a smartphone for repair. What you must keep in mind is that if you were to bring your phone for repair by any non-official repair person or shop, any active manufacturer warranty may be voided. Additionally, if the smartphone has some type of special waterproof feature, it is safe to assume that you no longer have it after a third-party repair.

A TYPICAL AFTERMARKET IPHONE SCREEN REPLACEMENT KIT

In any case, before bringing it a phone (or any device for that matter) in for repair by anyone, it is a good practice to make a backup of your data as described in the previous section.

When you bring your device in for repair services, read any service agreement or contract, and ask all the questions about pricing and fees. Before committing, go to a common online retailer, like Amazon.com or eBay.com, to see how much a **refurbished** or a functional used phone of the exact model costs. If the total cost of repair comes close to or exceeds the prices you see, then you should reconsider if the repair is worthwhile.

Chapter 6

Smart Things

The common everyday appliances around us will continue to be computerized and digitized. From the thermostat to the vacuum cleaner to even the microwave oven, we are now in the age where common day appliances are also connected to the Internet.

Wearables is the term used to describe the category where we find **smartwatches,** which picked up momentum in the 2010s, although they have been around earlier than that. Apple's popular **Watch** can allow you to make and take phone calls (with an additional fee on top of your monthly bill). At the time of writing, the Watch itself runs from about

$400 to $1,400 for one that is co-branded with Hermès.

Smart TVs are also become commonplace. Most of the TVs built by Samsung, LG, Sony, and others have an operating system built-in that allows you connect your TV to the Internet so you can watch your favorite flick on Netflix or Hulu. Look at the back of the TV where the ports are and you will likely find a port for network, sometimes labeled LAN.

Other **smart home devices** are also proliferating like rabbits. There are now computerized devices that can control the temperature of your house, vacuum your house and remember the floor plan, and turn lights on and off.

Few of these smart home devices (that some can be classified under what the industry calls **IoT** or the **Internet of Things**) have critical life-sustaining functionality but they sure bring a lot of convenience (or maybe laziness, depending on how you see it.)

THIS SMART POWER PLUG ALLOWS YOU TO POWER APPLIANCES ON AND OFF BY USING VOICE COMMANDS WITH A VOICE ASSISTANT LIKE GOOGLE ASSISTANT.

One can argue that there may be truly useful reason for such devices. For example, if you have difficulty standing up and down because of a knee injury, being able to voice command lights to go on or off is indeed convenient.

One of the most popular smart home devices are **smart doorbells with cameras**. There are many on the market but the one that is the most popular is the **Ring Video Doorbell**. The other options are Netgear **Arlo** and **Nest Hello**. These are designed to replace (or work with) your conventional doorbell with a video camera and Internet capabilities.

How do these things work? Let's take the Ring doorbell as an example. The Ring doorbell behaves like any other doorbell, but it sends a notification to your smartphone or some other device when someone gets close to the door or when someone presses the doorbell button.

When you get the notification, you have the choice to view a live video feed of who might be in front of the door. If you choose to, you can tap a button to communicate with the person at the door. Now, because this happens over the Internet, you don't have to be home to receive the notifications. Yes, that means that while you are vacationing in Orlando, you can see who is at your front door in Seattle.

Voice assistants

The major tech companies now have some version of a voice assistant. The first mainstream **voice assistant** was launched by Apple in their iPhones and iPads in 2011. They called "her" **Siri**. Microsoft would later launch **Cortana**, named after a character in their popular *Halo* Xbox game. Amazon calls theirs **Alexa** and it is probably the most widely used. Google, too, has a voice assistant called **Google Assistant.**

Fun Fact: You can tell Amazon's Alexa to sing Happy Birthday, meow, fart, clap, and even tell you a knock-knock joke.

The most common way to use these voice assistants is through a small powered device (about the size of a soda can) that sits on your countertop or on your desk. As an example,

Amazon sells a family of these **smart speakers** called *Echo* and a smaller version called *Echo Dot*. Google has a similar pair offering called *Google Home* and *Google Home Mini*. To use these smart speakers, you will need to use a word or phrase to "wake" it up before asking it to do something. For Amazon's Echo, it's *"Alexa"* or *"Echo"*. For Google's Home, it's *"Hey Google"*.

AMAZON'S SMART SPEAKER LINE, ECHO (LEFT) AND ECHO DOT (RIGHT)

Think of these voice assistants as just a capability for you to *speak* what you are searching for instead of typing it into a computer. One major difference between these voice assistance and simple search is that in addition to performing searches on the Internet, they can also be connected to other smart home devices that will understand and perform simple commands like turning an appliance on and off.

This a typical and simple setup: you set up an Amazon's Echo Dot with Alexa and you install with a smart light bulb in the bedroom and set it up with a name like "bedroom lights". After making sure that the Alexa app on your phone can detect the light bulb, you can now say "Alexa, turn bedroom lights on". Boom! Like magic, the light turns on.

If you get past the question of whether you *really* need a digital assistant at home with a yes, the next question will be which one. The two horses in the race are Amazon's Alexa or

Google Assistant. At the time of writing, Amazon is taking the lead, but Google's product is gaining momentum in market share.

What will help you make your decision is asking what you want to use it for. If you merely want ask trivia questions, then either one is fine. If you want to control smart home gadgets installed in the house, then you will have to do a little research to determine if the voice platform is compatible with the gadgets you need. You will see gadgets and appliances described as "works with Alexa" or "works with Google Home". Many will work with both.

Chapter 7

The Internet

Most, if not all, of the technology described here rely on the Internet. Think of the Internet as a bunch of computers connected around the world. The magic starts when you ask what you can do with that incredible network.

Some of these connected computers hold information or data that other people are interested in seeing, like current news, recipes, or funny cat videos. When the Internet is used to get to information like that, some prefer to call that *World Wide Web* (abbreviated WWW). For most purposes, both are used interchangeably.

These computers are typically call **servers** and typically there are not just one server that hosts the content that you are looking for. For a website that has a lot of visitor traffic, we're probably talking thousands of servers. For the website of your local pet store, probably one server would suffice.

No one or any single entity owns the Internet, but depending on where you live, there may be restrictions and censorship placed by the local authorities. There is no way to legally access Facebook, for example, inside of China.

You can access the Internet using a variety of means and it's all the same Internet regardless of how you connect to the Internet. Typically, at home, you would have a monthly subscription with a residential **ISP** or **Internet Service Provider**, like Comcast in the United States. The ISPs will likely have a physical hardware in (or on top of) your home. Typically, this is a **modem**.

This modem may carry TV and phone signals as well as Internet network signals. You would typically connect an ethernet cable from the back of the modem and to the back of your computer, or more commonly, if you have a laptop, connect wirelessly through **Wi-Fi** or a wireless signal.

Many public places and establishments, like McDonalds, Starbucks, libraries, airports, malls, etc. have free wireless network you can use. What you need to do is to choose the **SSID** (or simply, a network signal) that is made available at that location and join your device to the network.

There is a good chance that your browser may automatically appear and redirect you to a page to have you agree to their terms of use or show you some short video ads. This is very common. What is uncommon is if you are asked you to create accounts, download an app, or provide personal information.

Search Engines and Browsers

Search engines, like **Google.com** or **Bing.com**, started as websites that help you find other websites that may contain information that you are looking for. These days, the search engines will give you the answers to what you are looking for without sending you to another website to see the answer. For example, typing "who is the richest person in the world" into Google will display answer without visiting another website.

Internet browsers, on the other hand, are software or apps that are installed on your laptop, desktop, phone, tablet, etc. that help you *browse* websites on the Internet. You would use a browser, like Chrome or Safari on an iPhone, to go to a search engine, like Google.com, to find out who is the richest person in the world.

To be clear, you don't need to go to a search engine just to get to a website. Each website has an address called **URL** (or unique resource locator) like *https://Amazon.com* or in marketing material, you may just see *Amazon.com*. Type any of these directly into the **address bar** of your browser.

The concluding '.com' part of a URL gives you some clue of the owners of and type of the website. The most common is *.com* and it indicates that it is a commercial entity. A *.gov* (like *WhiteHouse.gov*) tells you that it is a governmental entity. A *.edu* (like *Harvard.edu*) tells you it is an academic institution. A *.ca* (like *TimHortons.ca*) indicates that it is based in Canada.

There are too many of these **TLD** (top level domains), but when you see a TLD not matching up to what the business should be, you have every right to be suspicious.

Safe Browsing

Ever noticed that some website URLs start with **http** and some with **https**? Sometimes you will even see a lock icon next to address. In short, when you see the extra 's' (which stands for **secure**), it means that the website is using a secure means to send and receive information to your browser using something called **encryption**. You typically don't have to worry about setting up your browser to use encryption, since it is automatic.

When you use a browser on your computer to visit a website, information makes its way through several routers and servers before finally reaching its destination. Network engineers call machine-to-machine paths **hops**.

Fun Fact: When I tested how many hops it takes my browser to reach Amazon.com, after 10 hops, I am still inside of Comcast's network!

We frequently type in sensitive information, like passwords, credit card numbers, personal information, etc. into a website to get to some information or make a purchase. At or in between any two machines, a hacker can intercept the message heading somewhere and look at that information. This sort of malicious interception is creatively called *MITM* or *Man-in-the-Middle* attacks. No, really. However, when it is encrypted, that information will be all gibberish and useless.

The guidance here is to not enter information that you don't want a stranger to see into a website that is not using **https** in the URL.

Internet Service Providers

These days, it is not uncommon to have multiple devices in the home that need to be connected to the Internet. Other than desktops, laptops, tablets, phones, and peripherals like printers, some smart home appliances these days also need to be "connected", especially wirelessly.

Typically, your ISP (such as Comcast) will not charge you a subscription based on how many devices you will connect. They may make a recommendation, but they usually don't charge by devices to be connected.

How they charge their subscription is really based on the **upload** and **download** speeds you want, and sometimes how much data you may need to upload and download. At the time of writing, Comcast, as an example, offers most of their customers, a 1TB per month plan, which equals about watching about 700 hours of high definition video. That's around 20 hours a day of Netflix!

Router & Access Point

If you have two desktops and a printer at home that need to be connected to the Internet, you are going to need to plug an ethernet cable into each of them and then plug the other end into the back of the modem that your ISP provide. Chances are the modem will not have enough network ports and this is where a **router** comes in.

A ROUTER WHICH ALSO FUNCTIONS AS WIRELESS ACCESS POINT.

A router is like a power strip. It takes one signal and splits it into multiple ones. Additionally, most routers also function as a **wireless access point** which broadcasts at least one wireless signal so that your devices can get a network connection wirelessly as well. Most modem provided by your ISP functions as a wireless access point as well.

The signals broadcasted by a router or your modem have limited range. Think of these signals as a small, concentric, and limited radio signals. Indoors, these wireless signals theoretically spread 150 feet out (like a sphere) but walls and other physical obstructions limit its reach. The best thing you can do is to have the router as centrally-located as possible in your house.

It is very common to see your neighbors' network signals if the houses are built fairly close together… and yes, they can see yours too. Well, can't some unscrupulous neighbors just use your wireless signal instead of paying for their own?

Technically, yes but they shouldn't be able to if you have set a **password** or **passphrase** for your modem and your wireless signal. Typically, you will see terms like WEP, WPA, WPA2, etc. These are security technologies to protect your password for your wireless signal. Look at the manual or ask for assistance to set a password. Many routers have default usernames and passwords set – this doesn't mean you're all set! These devices all come out of the box with the same default login and password, so you are going to need to set your own.

Chapter 8

Email & Messaging

Gone are the days when you pen a letter and after sending it in the mail, hope that it gets to your recipient in a few days, and then another few more days for a response, provided your recipient doesn't procrastinate responding!

Invented in the 1990s, **email** or **electronic mail** is by far the most commonly used mode of written communication these days. Most ISPs, like Comcast, give their customers an email address when they become subscribers, but you are neither obligated to use that nor should you pay any money to get another email account.

For personal use, there is nearly no reason to pay for a new email account. They are free. Some of the more popular email services include Google's *Gmail* and Microsoft's *Hotmail*. There are probably hundreds more free email services out there.

Getting a new email account from Gmail and Hotmail is easy, but you will likely need to verify your identity by providing a mobile number. Almost none will ask for more sensitive personal information like your address, social security number, etc.

There are no restrictions on getting and using more than one email account from a single email provider (if you are up for managing a bunch of email accounts) or having one of each from each provider if you like. All you will need is to find a **username** or **alias** that is not already taken. Your entire email address will be your username, the @ symbol, and the **domain name** like this: bob@hotmail.com

On that note, you can almost certainly forget about trying 'bob' or 'sally' as usernames. These are likely taken early on because people view them as a commodity or status. For the same reason, many first name-last name combinations, like 'JohnSmith' are likely taken too. They aren't stealing your identity, they just happen to have the same first and last name. Most likely, you will end up adding something before or after your name or something unique.

After you have an email account, you can read and send email via several methods and on a variety of devices. Suppose you have a Hotmail email account, in addition to using the browser, you can use an email program (or sometimes called **client**), like Outlook or Mail, to send and receive email messages. Additionally, you can set up another email app on your phone to check the same email as well. When a new email message arrives, both email programs on different devices will get the message.

Most conveniently and for most email services, you can check your email using any Internet browser installed on a device that is connected to the Internet. This means that so long as you can find a device that has Internet access (except for countries with restrictions) you will be able to get to your email: in a public library in Orlando to a Starbucks in London to an Internet café in the Philippines.

Spam

Not to be confused with the delicious canned meat loved by Hawaiian locals, **spam** refers to unsolicited email messages that are sent to you. In fact, it doesn't take much for you to receive spam email messages. The thing to keep in mind is that when you receive a spam email message, chances are you are one of thousands, if not millions, receiving it. The fact that you are receiving spam does not mean that your machine or device is infected with a virus or you have been hacked. Most of these are harmless (but annoying) marketing messages. There will be some that are more malicious and we'll talk about that later.

Most email services will try to detect spam messages and direct them into a **spam or junk folder**. Such anti-spam systems aren't perfect as some legitimate messages do get flagged and chucked into the spam or junk folder. It pays to take a glance at that folder occasionally.

Spam messages will appear like it is personalized to you and sometimes may even address you by your first name, but there are tell-tale signs of these unsolicited messages. For example, many will congratulate you or tell you earned a discount or prize. Others will use characters that look like actual letters to spell out a word to avoid getting detected by anti-spam systems.

A good advice is to never click "unsubscribe" - it only confirms to the sender that the email address is real and active. Just ignore them.

My recommendation is to get a free email (Gmail, Hotmail, etc.) and use that consistently to register at websites, make purchases, subscriptions, sign up for newsletter, etc. That account can then get slammed with the inevitable junk. Then create one for other services and accounts that you use regularly, like bills, utility portals, payment portals, etc.

Hacked Email?

Possible but unlikely if we are just talking about spam. Chances are your email wasn't not hacked into but it is just receiving a lot of spam emails. Simply put, your email address just made it to several hundred or thousand undesirable **mailing lists**.

There is, of course, a chance that an email was sent to you with the intent to plant a virus in your computer. These are almost always email messages that have some form of attachment (a PDF file, a Word document, etc.) that they want you to click and open. Others will want you to go to a website to see some information. We'll cover these malicious nuisances in a later chapter. Never open an attachment in an unexpected email, even if it seems to come from someone you know.

There is, of course, a possibility that someone has really "hacked" into your email account. There are ways to protect yourself from someone using your stolen username and password to log into your email account. One approach is called *multi-factor authentication*. We'll cover that in a later chapter as well.

Messaging and Chat

Using the power of the Internet to communicate in real time is not new. In late 1980s and 1990s, many used something called *IRC* (or Internet Relay Chat) to chat in real time.

These days, there are several popular chat and messaging apps and services. Some are part of another larger service or platform, such as Facebook and Twitter, and others are standalones, such as Snapchat or WhatsApp. The capabilities of these messaging platforms now have grown well past simple text when IRC was invented, to sending pictures, videos, and audio messages.

One limitation in these messaging services is that typically two parties must be on the same messaging platforms in order for them to communicate. For example, if you have an iPhone, you have a messaging service that is unique to Apple called **iMessage**.

Unfortunately, you can only use iMessage to communicate with someone who also has an iPhone or an Apple product. A friend with an Android phone will not be able to receive or send you messages using iMessage since it is proprietary to Apple. Just to make it confusing to new iPhone users, your regular text messages and iMessage messages appear in the same Message app, each sporting a different color.

Yes, there are apps out there that will function to aggregate and manage all your messaging apps, if that is a must-have for you. As a caveat though, all are missing the ability to add one of the most popular messaging platforms used today – iMessage.

We cannot finish this chapter without quickly mentioning about **Snapchat**. What made Snapchat famous and popular among very young users is a feature that makes messages only readable for a short time. These days, one of Snapchat's most used feature is called *Lenses*, which allows users to superimpose realistic-looking special effects in real-time video chatting, like making yourself look like a puppy or swap faces with another person.

Fun fact: Here's a list of some popular abbreviations used in Snapchat in case you find yourself snooping around, shopping for a heart attack, and attempting to decipher some text message. Sorry kids.

2nite: tonight
bff: best friends forever
bf/gf: boyfriend or girlfriend
brb: be right back
cd9: code 9, parents are around
gnoc: get naked on camera
irl: in real life
lh6: let's have sex
lmk: let me know
np: no problem or nosy parents
pos: parents over shoulder
stfu: shut the fuck up
ttyl: talk to you later
wyd: what you doing

Chapter 9

Social Networks

With the power of the Internet, we can now stay connected and the choices by which we stay connected are as varied as the type of bread you find at the grocery store. There are "multigrain" ones and plain ones, casual ones and professional ones. You pick.

Facebook

Who hasn't heard of **Facebook**?

Well, there are some I am sure. Facebook is the world's most popular **social network**.

Each Facebook user has an account that is connected to other user accounts of friends and family, for example. This forms the basic network. On top of this people connection are other networks of common causes, interests, belief systems, hobbies, movies, music bands… and yes, political affiliations!

How someone can use Facebook can fill several books, so this is not the right book for that. At the time of writing in 2018, Facebook has been in the news a lot and for reasons that we won't go into. Read the concluding section of this chapter if you are considering creating an account with any social network.

Twitter

Twitter is another large social network that allows their users to post and read what they call **tweets** or 280-character messages. Tweets often contain with callouts to topics with the use of **hashtags**, *#ToyStory4*, such as "Just saw a trailer for #ToyStory4 and it looks awesome!" The idea behind using hashtag is that if you are interested in learning what everyone on *Twitterverse* has to say about *Toy Story 4*, you can search for tweets by the *#ToyStory4* hashtag.

Tweets are typically more intended to be read by a large number of users called **followers**. You *follow* people to see their tweets, and people follow you to see your tweets. Like what you read? You can *like* or *retweet* their message. A Twitter username is preceded by the at symbol: *@LadyGaga* or *@ChickfilA*.

Fun fact: To pack as much text into a tweet, abbreviations and contractions are commonly used. Here're some popular just in case you need to use them...

afaik: as far as I know
dm: direct message
fml: fuck my life
fwiw: for what it's worth
hth: hope that helps
imho: in my honest opinion
imo: in my opinion

j/k: just joking

lmao: laughing my ass off

lol: laughing out loud

rt: retweet

stfu: shut the fuck up

The number of followers is some sort of popularity gauge. Seven of the top 10 Twitter users with the highest number of users are all megastar musicians or entertainers. Each of the current top three—Katy Perry, Justin Bieber, and Barack Obama—has over 100 million followers at the end of 2018.

Instagram

With over a billion users, **Instagram** is another social network that you will hear a lot of. Owned by Facebook, Instagram's bread-and-butter is the sharing of meaningful photos and videos posted by users. Instagram offers several image filters that allow users to visually modify their photos, like an aged and dramatic look using the *Toaster* filter, or a dusty and vintage look using the *Reyes* filter.

Others

There are other social networks that have specific purposes, such as **LinkedIn** for professional network and **Pinterest** for managing ideas and interests using images. In many ways, **YouTube** is also a social network and a pretty lucrative one with millions of subscribers.

What you need to know

So, which social network do you need?

Well, the first question should really be if you need one at all. For someone who is on the job market, being on LinkedIn is more useful above all other social networks. If you are somewhat of an influencer and people care a lot about what you have to say, Twitter is a great option. Do a lot of travelling or love to share beautiful photos, choose Instagram instead. Facebook has been a perennial favorite for connecting with family and friends.

In any of these social networks, privacy of your data is a concern. Since most, if not all, are free to join and use, the platforms need to find a way to keep the lights on. How do they do that? Primarily ads.

A quick explanation of how ads will help you understand why people are up in arms about Facebook and potentially other social networks soon.

Social Networks and Ads

Any group—from a small business selling trinkets to Hollywood studio promoting a movie to a real estate agent trying to attract customers—needs to have some confidence that a social platform can target specific type of users that they like. The good news for these groups is that many social networks do have plenty of information about their users.

Don't throw your shoe quite yet!

When you sign up for an account, you like clicked a box that indicates that you agree to some 50,000-word *Terms of Service* or some *End User License Agreement* (or EULA) printed in fine print, which allows the social networks to collect and keep some information about you. The more defining information the social network has about their users, the more these groups are willing to pay for their ads to be displayed. If you own or have owned a business that benefits from some online marketing, chances are you will be 100% onboard with this practice.

Since Facebook is already taking so much flak in recent months, let's take Twitter as an example. If you follow mostly country singers on Twitter, and Goldenvoice wants to ramp up ticket sales for Stagecoach the leading country music festival, you shouldn't be surprised to see Stagecoach ads appearing when you browse through tweets in Twitter.

This is not a new marketing tactic. The TV commercials you see between segment of a program show are highly curated and targeted as well. Let's just say that you are not going to see commercials for Black & Decker power tools in between segments of *The Young and the Restless*.

Chapter 10

Maintenance & Servicing

Just like any appliances, computers can run into problems. The most common issue computer owners face is degrading performance: the desktop or laptop just ain't running as fast as before.

Slow computers can be a result of a few things. Remember that the computer is in the business of moving, reading, and writing data. When the computer is instructed to move too much data at one time, it will, by design, slow things down.

As an analogy, a typical moving company can help move a family into a new home in a reasonable amount of time. However, when 100 families decide that they all want to move out on the same day, the moving company can still operate but it will need to more time to complete one job in order to get to the next.

Frequently, you are not the one who is haphazardly giving the computer multiple tasks. Subtle tasks, called **background tasks**, are commonly triggered by the operating system or by some software that you may not be aware of. Some newly-installed app, **add-on**, or **widget** may also be designed to use background tasks to do things like fetching latest coupons from the Internet or checking the weather every 5 minutes. When these tasks get gratuitous, people like to call the software that uses them *bloatware*.

Many of these **bloatware** aren't even installed by you and come pre-installed with the computer out of the box, or are installed along with the installation of another app. Every bloatware will use some memory, network, or storage resource from your computer. One or a few is fine, but that starts to become a problem when all of them simultaneously want to use the computer's limited resources, especially its memory. If you don't need it or never asked for it, uninstall bloatware.

A second reason why your computer could be slow could be that the app or software (or a newer version of it) that you installed is demanding more resources. How does this happen?

Like appliances, which are designed to work with certain amount of power consumption, temperature, etc., a software program is also designed to work with certain memory allowance other requirements. The remedy here is either run an older version of the program or upgrade your hardware.

While memory is the biggest culprit in causing computers to be slow, another less obvious reason for slow computers has to do with storage. Remember I mentioned that the computer is in the business of moving data. When some software starts and runs, the computer needs to temporarily take up some disk space to allow the software to run normally. If there aren't enough temporary disk space, the app will either not start, run very slowly, or have every erratic behavior. iPads, for example, can start to have really unpredictable behaviors when it starts to run really low on storage space.

The remedy here is to free up storage space by uninstalling apps you don't need and deleting files that you don't need or want, like older pictures and videos.

Other computer problems

When a computer or some app doesn't run as expected, the easiest thing to try is to check if all the cables are connected properly. If the computer (especially a desktop) has been recently relocated or shifted, check to make sure that no cable connectors have been accidentally disconnected.

If the problem started occurring after a new software or hardware (like a new printer, webcam, etc.) was installed, remove the newly installed item to see if the problem goes away.

Cross-checking if other devices are having the same symptoms can also help you pinpoint what might be going on. Suppose your Internet browser on your laptop is suddenly not reaching any website. If you have an iPad at home and the tablet is also not showing any website, then you have an Internet connectivity issue.

If other devices can connect to the Internet, then issue is isolated to a problem on your computer or device. The logical next thing to try is to power it down (if possible) and power it back up. Many modern computer systems are designed to perform maintenance checks and (sometimes) repairs when they start or *boot* up. This is an easy thing to try for peripherals, especially routers, printers, etc.

Second thing to try is perform the "softest" possible reset or re-installation (if applicable). Softest here means the least intrusive or destructive step that you can take to get the device back to an operational state. Some devices like phones and tablets have a specific way to do a **soft reset** which typically involves pressing two or more buttons simultaneously. For most iPhones and iPads, for example, you can perform a soft reset by holding the power button and the home button until the device reboots.

Some software programs provide a choice for you to **reinstall or repair** the software while preserving your data. If there is not much data to save, like an Internet browser, you can always **uninstall and reinstall** it to see if it corrects the problem.

Many devices come a way to perform a **factory reset** that is NOT a "soft" reset. A factory reset will theoretically bring the phone back to day you took it out of the box, which means your data and settings will be erased. Most gadgets and devices might also come with an actual reset button or a pinhole that hides a reset button. Whether this is a hard reset (like a factory reset) or a soft reset depends on the device, so find the directions in the user manual or look it up on the Internet.

In any case, always backup or make a copy of your data before attempting any remedy step or bring it to any repair shop or person.

Service Plans

There is very few reasons why you should be paying an annual or monthly fee for some business, person, or app to maintain your home computer. Just as you won't give more than 5 seconds to someone who comes up to you at the parking lot to sell you brake pads or service your car, you shouldn't be considering any business that comes to you (via email, pop-up, phone call, letter, fax, postcard, etc.) and offer computer maintenance services, anti-virus protection, etc.

Professional services do not bargain or lower their prices. If the computer maintenance business is legit (like *Geek Squad*, etc.), they will unlikely bargain, or lower their fees to give you a "you-sound-like-a-nice-person" discount. Individually-operated or small shops may because you are a repeat customer, student, etc., but a reputable company will arbitrarily NOT lower their fees for a service.

You should NEVER pay anything upfront without a clear explanation what the deposit is used for. Computer services don't operate like home construction - they don't need 50% down to buy the raw material. A ballpark estimate should be agreed upon and payment due when work is completed as agreed. Some places may charge a small initial fee to make an initial assessment of what might be wrong with your faulty device.

Very importantly, most computer servicing and repairs are NOT done remotely over the phone or Internet by someone you do not know. While this is common at a business with an in-house or contracted IT support team, remote technical support by a stranger is not something that is advisable for residential settings.

Unless it is your tech savvy nephew or your IT department, do NOT let anyone remotely log into your computer, click around your desktop to perform checks, maintenance, or repairs. These should ideally be done in person or brought to the technician or shop.

There are, of course, simple maintenance that you can perform by yourself. For example, that humming from your desktop comes from one or more fans that are designed to cool the desktop while it is running. Over time, these fans can get louder or may even produce a low pitch squeal. If that annoys you, you'll be happy to know that chances are they are replaceable. If the desktop got suddenly got nice and quiet one day, don't be too happy. There is a chance that the fan malfunctioned and now components inside the desktop will start to overheat.

ONE OF MANY FANS THAT KEEPS COMPONENTS COOL IN A DESKTOP.

It is very common for a layer of dust to form on parts of the desktop, typically where there is airflow. This is easily remedied with a can of compressed air and a vacuum cleaner. With the appropriate gear to prevent the dust from finding your face or food, spray bursts of air into the desktop and slurp up it with a vacuum cleaner.

Chapter 11

Malware & Viruses

Viruses are really computer programs that are intentionally designed to "infect" your computer for one or more specific destructive or malicious purpose.

Malware and viruses should be distinguished from **bugs** which are unintended programming errors in an app or some other software that cause unexpected behavior. An app that used to start and run just fine, but now shuts unexpectedly or even predictably is likely the outcome of a bug or a hardware problem, not a virus.

That said, virus creators frequently use software bugs to make their viruses work. These bugs are frequently called **vulnerabilities**. Software and operating system makers will frequently provide free updates to correct these issues, which is why it is important that your operating system and software are up-to-date.

Why a virus was created and what task it is programmed to do varies. Some are out of mischief, but most have a more malicious intent, such as to secretly record your keystrokes on the keyboard to find your passwords, or monitor your purchase transactions to steal your credit card information.

Others, which may not fit the exact definition of a virus, are actually installed by reputable companies to monitor your online behavior so that they can target you with ads or sell your information to others. This is definitely a grey area because many websites do track your online behavior.

For example, if you were to go to eBay and look up *'flower bouquets'*, don't be surprised if you were to see ads from eBay in another website that are conveniently showing you flower bouquets. This is called **retargeting** in the business.

Ransomware

In recent years, some hackers have been exploiting a Wi-Fi-related vulnerability and appears to have the ability to perform a **ransomware** - where they lock up your device and data unless you somehow pay a ransom. Just as you should always know where your spare tire is, you should always know where your backup contents are. If you become a victim of ransomware, just reset your device to factory defaults and put the saved contents back in.

This really reinforces the practice of backing up data. Make copies or back up files (photos, documents, etc.) you don't want to lose *in* your device *out of* your device into an external location like an external hard disk drive, USB stick (also known as flash drives) or cloud storage. It is not illegal to store 3 copies of your wedding or baby pictures in different locations!

Cloud storage is becoming a popular option. If you have Hotmail, you already have free 5GB of storage on *OneDrive*. There are plenty of other free cloud storage out there: Dropbox, Google Drive, etc.

Scams & Phishing

Microsoft or any big reputable tech or non-tech company will almost never call or email you about an issue that needs your *immediate* attention: accounts locked, need verification, computer needs an update, fraud detection, etc. There are too many users to individually worry about. If anything happens, you'll find out and you're going need to call them to resolve it.

If you receive an email supposedly from Google, Amazon, Apple, PayPal, Microsoft, etc., look the actual email address (not the displayed name) or the link they want you to click on. Chances are it doesn't have an Amazon.com or Microsoft.com in it. That's what they call **phishing**. Phishing is a way scammers and hackers (typically over email) get you to believe that they are legit in order to get your information (password, credit card info, etc.)

Oh, check the grammar of the email message. You can safely assume that if an email is legitimately coming from Apple or Microsoft, it will contain misspellings, run-on sentences, dangling participles, and other grammatical mistakes. Take a look the following text from an email I received recently. Does it look like it came from Apple?

Policy Violation

Immediate action required: Your Apple ID is being suspended

Dear sseow@hotmail.com,

We have recently detected that your Apple ID has been having an issue with your billing account. We are unable to verify the billing information you provided. Your Apple ID has been suspended and a notification has been send to the billing Account owner. Please work with them in order to resolve the issue.

We will delete your Apple ID unless the billing owner corrects the violation by filling out the Account Verification From within three business days. This from verifies your identity and ownership of the payment instrument. Failure to provide the requested documents may result in permanent account closure Click Account Verification From to the resolved issue.

Sincerely,

Apple Account Team

TM and Copyright © 2018 Apple Inc. 1 Infinite Loop, Cuportino Ca 95014 United States.

Where is *Cuportino*?

Scammers will continue to get creative because old concepts, like the Nigerian prince one, get old. It is impossible to predict what would be the next narrative but they all seem to appeal to whatever emotional centers you have that will make you open your wallet.

Chapter 12

Security & Passwords

Using a combination of username and password is the most common way online services **authenticate** or check to make sure we are authorized to get to an account or get to data.

Usernames are typically selected by you and has to be unique in that no one else has used it. Some services may use your email address or telephone as the username or user id. Most systems will not like spaces and some special characters like the % sign.

Passwords or PIN (if it is entirely numbers) are also typically set by the user and most will have requirements for the *complexity* of the password to prevent hackers from using a *brute force* method to guess your password. Most will require at least 8 characters and may want you to include uppercase characters, lowercase characters, numbers, and special symbols like "!" or "_".

Multi-Factor Authentication

In order to make it a little harder for someone to get into your account in the event that they guessed the correct username and password, or successfully stole them, security experts have implemented an additional security measure called **multi-factor authentication** (abbreviated **MFA**) or **2-factor authentication** (abbreviated **2FA**).

When you have MFA or 2FA enabled, say for your email access, when anyone (including you) tries to use your username and password to log into your email account, the email service will perform addition steps to verify your identity, typically using text messaging. You will receive a text message that contains a code (typically numerical) at your registered mobile number that you will have to type into the login screen. This means that if you were to receive a text message with a code unexpectedly, someone may be trying to log into your account. The immediate action that you should take is to log into your account and change your password.

Fun Fact: Yes, researchers know the most commonly-used passwords. In other words, if your password resembles any of these, for the love of God, change it to something else. Here's the top 25 passwords in 2018:

123456
password
123456789
12345678
12345
111111
1234567
sunshine

qwerty
iloveyou
princess
admin
welcome
666666
abc123
football
123123
monkey
654321
!@#$%^&*
charlie
aa123456
donald
password1
qwerty123

Chapter 13

New & Shiny

Every month, something new is invented and introduced to the market. Some will take time before they become mainstream (like bendable smartphone screens) but others may have already changed the way we do things.

Cloud

I've used the term 'cloud' several times in the book and surely you have heard the term in packaging and ads. So, what on Earth is the cloud?

Cloud just really means a location for storing data other than your computer at home. You can buy and install a **Network Attached**

Storage (abbreviated **NAS)** that can function like an external Hard Disk Drive to hold backups of your data or music and video files. That is not quite *cloud*, even if it may be branded as *My Cloud*.

When you save some data in the cloud, you may be saving in a server physically located in a remote location. It could be in saved in one of 50,000 servers in a large **server farm** located in North Dakota for example.

The advantage of saving something in the cloud is that professional cloud storage services always save multiple duplicates of your data. If your computer goes kaput, your data may be lost forever if you don't have another copy. If your data is saved in the cloud and the server holding your data goes down (because of a power failure or the entire server farm gets leveled by an earthquake), they'll simply retrieve the duplicate copies. Let's just say it will take a pretty coordinated effort to make them lose all copies of your data.

Bitcoin

Bitcoin is one of many and the leading **cryptocurrencies** available today. Simply put, cryptocurrency is digital money. Bitcoin, specifically, was created in response to the financial crisis in 2008. The creator or creators (going by the name *Satoshi Nakamoto*) of Bitcoin remain unknown today but its growth has been impressive. The cryptocurrency's value peaked at almost $20,000 in December of 2017 but have since dropped.

What sets Bitcoin apart from the cash system that we know and use is the concept that the *ledger* (or records of financial transactions) is not kept and privately managed by one single institution (your bank). In Bitcoin, the ledger is public, decentralized, and duplicated across over 10,000 computers (at the time of writing). All transactions are known and verified by these computers called **nodes**.

And once verified, it becomes nearly impossible to alter the transaction record.

What makes cryptocurrencies so tamper-proof is a type of data technology called **blockchain**. Bitcoin just happen to be the most popular use of blockchain. There are other uses of blockchain that doesn't involve cryptocurrency. In many instances where it is integral to keep an accurate and trustworthy record of some commodity or something of value, blockchain can useful.

The only ways to own Bitcoin or other cryptocurrencies is for someone to send you some, earning them, or purchasing them in a cryptocurrency exchange very much like how you would do it for real stocks. Cryptocurrencies live in **digital wallets** that you own or with the trading platform you use. In other words, cryptocurrencies do NOT exist in any other form, like paper or metallic coins. In fact, you can own fractions of one

Bitcoin, like 0.05 and do not need buy a whole single Bitcoin.

Artificial Intelligence

A definite buzzword in the tech industry today. The definition of **artificial intelligence** (abbreviated **AI**) is muddied with how Hollywood portrays human-annihilating AI, what really clever scientists and tech companies build that "has" AI, and what marketers proclaim to be AI that is making a product superior to others.

In many cases, AI just turns out to be a really sophisticated code that can perform certain tasks that humans can do but perhaps faster or better. Doing something impressively faster or better, like complex calculations and computations, however, doesn't quite qualify as AI.

Personally, the day I can tell a computer a joke and make it laugh uncontrollably, or have it detect sarcasm or irony is the day I will start worrying about AI. In the meantime, I'll enjoy having Alexa tell me jokes and the kids will safely continue having her make flatulence sounds.

Index

gigabyte, 26
Gmail, 10, 86, 90
Google, 9, 22
Google Assistant,
  71
Google Drive, 117
Google Home, 71
Google Home Mini,
  71
grammar, 118
hackers, 19, 116,
  118
Halo, 70
hard disk drives, 27
hard drive, 25
hard reset, 109
hashtags, 96
HDD, 25
HDMI, 35
Hermès, 67
Hey Google, 71
hops, 79
Hotmail, 86, 90,
  117
https, 79, 80
Hulu, 67
iCloud, 9, 62

iMac Pro, 55
iMacs, 20
iMessage, 92
Instagram, 98
Internet, 74
Internet browsers,
  77
Internet café, 88
Internet of Things,
  67
Internet Relay Chat,
  91
Internet Service
  Provider, 75
iOS, 22
IoT, 67
iPads, 14, 22, 70,
  106, 108
iPhone, 9, 22, 61,
  63, 70, 92, 108
IRC, 91
ISP, 75
iTunes, 9, 61
jailbreak, 23
Jeff Bezos, 11
junk folder, 89
keystrokes, 115

Office 365, 7
OneDrive, 117
operating system,
  12
Outlook, 87
passphrase, 83
password, 83, 121
Paul Allen, 7
PC, 13
performance, 103
peripherals, 32
personal computer,
  13
phishing, 118
photos, 98
PIN, 121
Pinterest, 99
pixels, 36
Power, 34
Professional
  services, 110
RAM, 29
Random Access
  Memory, 29
ransomware, 116
Razer, 53
refurbished, 64

reinstall, 109
re-installation, 108
reset, 108
restore, 62
retargeting, 116
Reyes, 98
Ring Video
  Doorbell, 69
RJ11, 40
RJ45, 40
role-playing games,
  52
router, 82
RPG, 52
Safari, 77
Samsung, 56, 60
Sandisk, 62
Satoshi Nakamoto,
  127
scammers, 118
screen size, 36
search engine, 72
Sergey Brin, 9
server farm, 126
sideloading, 23
Siri, 70